Hands-On Dashboard Development with Shiny

A practical guide to building effective web applications and dashboards

Chris Beeley

BIRMINGHAM - MUMBAI

Hands-On Dashboard Development with Shiny

Commissioning Editor: Sunith Shetty
Acquisition Editor: Karan Jain
Content Development Editor: Karan Thakkar
Technical Editor: Sagar Sawant
Copy Editor: Safis Editing
Project Coordinator: Nidhi Joshi
Proofreader: Safis Editing
Indexer: Mariammal Chettiyar
Graphics: Jisha Chirayil
Production Coordinator: Shraddha Falebhai

First published: August 2018

Production reference: 1310818

Published by Packt Publishing Ltd.
Livery Place
35 Livery Street
Birmingham
B3 2PB, UK.

ISBN 978-1-78961-155-7

www.packtpub.com

`mapt.io`

Mapt is an online digital library that gives you full access to over 5,000 books and videos, as well as industry leading tools to help you plan your personal development and advance your career. For more information, please visit our website.

Why subscribe?

- Spend less time learning and more time coding with practical eBooks and Videos from over 4,000 industry professionals

- Improve your learning with Skill Plans built especially for you

- Get a free eBook or video every month

- Mapt is fully searchable

- Copy and paste, print, and bookmark content

Packt.com

Did you know that Packt offers eBook versions of every book published, with PDF and ePub files available? You can upgrade to the eBook version at `www.packt.com` and as a print book customer, you are entitled to a discount on the eBook copy. Get in touch with us at `customercare@packtpub.com` for more details.

At `www.packt.com`, you can also read a collection of free technical articles, sign up for a range of free newsletters, and receive exclusive discounts and offers on Packt books and eBooks.

Contributors

About the author

Chris Beeley is the author of *Web Application Development with R Using Shiny*. He has been using R and other open source software for 10 years to better capture, analyze, and visualize data in the healthcare sector in the UK. He works full-time developing software to store, collate, and present questionnaire data using open technologies (MySQL, PHP, R, and Shiny), with a special emphasis on using the web and Shiny to produce simple and attractive data summaries. He is attempting to expand the use of R and Shiny both within his own organization and throughout the rest of the health sector, as well as enabling his organization to better use a variety of other data science tools. He has also delivered talks about Shiny all over the country.

Packt is searching for authors like you

If you're interested in becoming an author for Packt, please visit `authors.packtpub.com` and apply today. We have worked with thousands of developers and tech professionals, just like you, to help them share their insight with the global tech community. You can make a general application, apply for a specific hot topic that we are recruiting an author for, or submit your own idea.

Table of Contents

Preface

Shiny is a framework for the R language that allows you to very easily produce powerful and attractive applications over the web. This allows your user to explore, analyze, and download data and analyses straight from their web browser. In this book, you will learn how to create flexible layouts and have full control over the layout of the dashboard and application.

This book helps you to create, reskin, and rebuild your application using methods such as HTML, CSS, JavaScript, and style sheets. You will learn how to produce dashboards using the Shiny command and dashboard package and how to use HTML templates and the Bootstrap framework. Finally, you will learn how to lay out applications using a wide range of built-in functions.

By the end of the book, you will have an understanding of the principles that underpin layout in Shiny applications, including sections of HTML added to a vanilla Shiny application, HTML interfaces written from scratch, dashboards, navigation bars, and interfaces.

Who this book is for

If you have some experience writing Shiny applications and want to use HTML, CSS, and Bootstrap to make custom interfaces, then this book is for you.

What this book covers

Chapter 1, *HTML and Shiny*, explains how to modify Shiny applications with built-in functions, HTML, and CSS. You will also learn how to create a application to download reports using R Markdown.

Chapter 2, *Layout Functions in Shiny*, covers the use of the Bootstrap framework and explains more about laying out your application. You will be building an application from scratch using Shiny Bootstrap-based functions.

Chapter 3, *Dashboards*, goes through the creation of dashboards using Shiny functions and the shiny dashboard package. We make use of notifications, messages, tasks, icons, and info boxes to build our dashboard.

To get the most out of this book

You require a basic knowledge of HTML, CSS, and RStudio, and vanilla Shiny installed on your system.

Download the example code files

You can download the example code files for this book from your account at www.packt.com. If you purchased this book elsewhere, you can visit www.packt.com/support and register to have the files emailed directly to you.

You can download the code files by following these steps:

1. Log in or register at www.packt.com
2. Select the **SUPPORT** tab
3. Click on **Code Downloads & Errata**
4. Enter the name of the book in the **Search** box and follow the onscreen instructions

Once the file is downloaded, please make sure that you unzip or extract the folder using the latest version of:

- WinRAR/7-Zip for Windows
- Zipeg/iZip/UnRarX for Mac
- 7-Zip/PeaZip for Linux

The code bundle for the book is also hosted on GitHub at https://github.com/PacktPublishing/Hands-On-Dashboard-Development-with-Shiny. In case there's an update to the code, it will be updated on the existing GitHub repository.

We also have other code bundles from our rich catalog of books and videos available at https://github.com/PacktPublishing/. Check them out!

Download the color images

We also provide a PDF file that has color images of the screenshots/diagrams used in this book. You can download it here: http://www.packtpub.com/sites/default/files/downloads/HandsOnDashboardDevelopmentwithShiny_ColorImages.pdf.

Conventions used

There are a number of text conventions used throughout this book.

`CodeInText`: Indicates code words in text, database table names, folder names, filenames, file extensions, pathnames, dummy URLs, user input, and Twitter handles. Here is an example: "The `dropdownMenu` function is used, to which is added the type, that is, the notification message or task."

A block of code is set as follows:

```
body = dashboardBody(
  fluidRow(
    infoBox("Average budget ($M)", 25, icon = icon("money"), color =
"green"),
    infoBoxOutput("infoBoxYear"),
    infoBoxOutput("infoBoxGenre")
  ),
```

Bold: Indicates a new term, an important word, or words that you see onscreen. For example, words in menus or dialog boxes appear in the text like this. Here is an example: "This is a **Linear** and **LOESS** translatable from each tab."

Warnings or important notes appear like this.

Tips and tricks appear like this.

Get in touch

Feedback from our readers is always welcome.

General feedback: If you have questions about any aspect of this book, mention the book title in the subject of your message and email us at `customercare@packtpub.com`.

Errata: Although we have taken every care to ensure the accuracy of our content, mistakes do happen. If you have found a mistake in this book, we would be grateful if you would report this to us. Please visit www.packt.com/submit-errata, selecting your book, clicking on the Errata Submission Form link, and entering the details.

Piracy: If you come across any illegal copies of our works in any form on the Internet, we would be grateful if you would provide us with the location address or website name. Please contact us at copyright@packt.com with a link to the material.

If you are interested in becoming an author: If there is a topic that you have expertise in and you are interested in either writing or contributing to a book, please visit authors.packtpub.com.

Reviews

Please leave a review. Once you have read and used this book, why not leave a review on the site that you purchased it from? Potential readers can then see and use your unbiased opinion to make purchase decisions, we at Packt can understand what you think about our products, and our authors can see your feedback on their book. Thank you!

For more information about Packt, please visit packt.com.

HTML and Shiny 1

Shiny is an R language framework that is used to create interactive and powerful web apps. Shiny can be used as a standalone app on a web page or as a build dashboard using R Markdown. This allows us to explore, download, and analyze data using a web browser. Shiny apps can be extended using CSS, JavaScript, and even an HTML widgets package.

In this chapter, we will be learning about Shiny built-in functions and HTML to build attractive, interactive, user-friendly applications. We will be covering the following topics in the chapter:

- Introducing Shiny functions to produce HTML
- Creating a Shiny app using HTML and CSS
- An application to download reports using R Markdown
- Introducing HTML templates

Shiny functions to produce HTML

Shiny is based on HTML and hence it allows you to write an entire interface in R and Shiny without thinking of HTML. You can also update your interface using Shiny built-in functions or add custom HTML using the `tag` function. Shiny also allows you to write an entire interface using HTML from scratch. To work on a Shiny application for the first time, it is preferable that you are familiar with HTML and CSS.

The following are a few common HTML tags:

- p: This is used to create a paragraph
- h1-h6: Heading style used to add headings and subheadings, where h1 is considered to be the largest and h6 the smallest
- a: This is used to create links and it is associated with href, which is the address to the web page. For example, href = http://shiny.rstudio.com/articles/, "Shiny docs", where href is used to define the link and the following text is used to display the text to the user
- br(): This is used to create a line break
- div: This tag is used to define a section with a particular style, defined in the same way as we use a div tag in HTML
- span: The span tag is used to define a similar style to a string of text
- pre: This is used for format code sections or commands in block quotes or pre-formatted text
- code: We can also use the code tag if you want the code block to look the same as computer code
- img: The img tag is used to define the image
- strong: This is used to set the text in bold format
- em: The em tag is used to style the text in italics format or to emphasize the text
- hr: This is used to add a horizontal line between text

The following screenshot shows the use of some of the HTML tags:

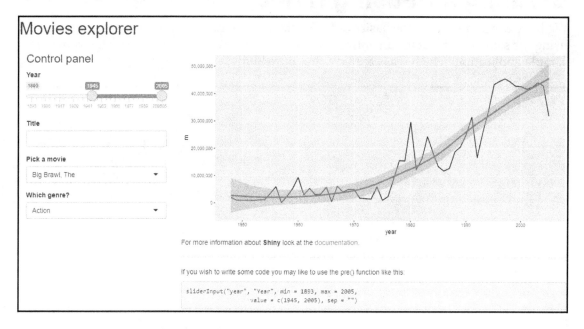

Let's have a look at the code for the application present in the ui.r file:

```
mainPanel(
    tabsetPanel(
        tabPanel("Budgets over time", plotOutput("budgetYear"),
            p("For more information about ", strong("Shiny"), " look at the
",
            a(href = "http://shiny.rstudio.com/articles/",
              "documentation.")),
            hr(),
            h3("Some code goes under here"),
            p("If you wish to write some code you may like to use the pre()
            function like this:",
            pre('sliderInput("year", "Year", min = 1893, max = 2005,
                value = c(1945, 2005), sep = "")'))),
        tabPanel("Movie picker", tableOutput("moviePicker"))
    )
)
```

As we can see in the code block, we have used a strong tag to add bold text within the p function within the same paragraph. We have also used href for the link, hr for the horizontal line, and the pre tag for the code block in the same application.

Creating a UI using HTML

We have covered some of the basics of HTML tags in the previous section. Here, we will be using the same tags to create an entire application using HTML. Let's review the previous sample application, which was created using pure Shiny:

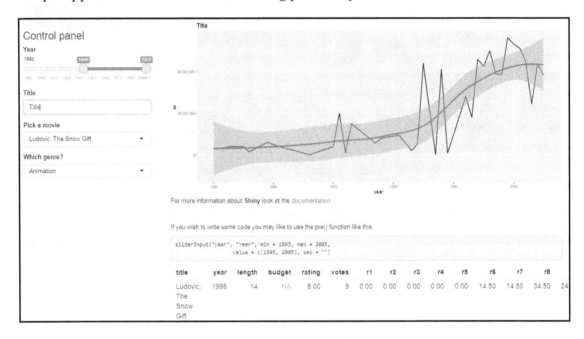

As you can see in the preceding screenshot, there are two drop-down boxes—one to select a movie title and one to select its genre. There is also a textbox, which is used to give a name to the graph. We will not be creating a range slider since producing a range slider using Shiny is much easier than using raw HTML. Here, our final output will be a graph, bold text, some links, and a table with some formatted code. Let's get started with the code part.

We will be adding the following three links in the `head` section; these are required to run the page correctly. You can add extra JavaScript and CSS links if you wish to use them in the application:

```
<script src="shared/jquery.js" type="text/javascript"></script>
<script src="shared/shiny.js" type="text/javascript"></script>
<link rel="stylesheet" type="text/css" href="shared/shiny.css"/>
```

The following link is a reference to the Bootstrap CSS, which is required to make columns and row `div` classes work correctly:

```
<link href="shared/bootstrap/css/bootstrap.min.css" rel="stylesheet">
```

We will be using more CSS later in this chapter.

Once the links are added, we will move on to the main body of the HTML. Add the following code block inside the `body` tag:

```
<h1>Minimal HTML UI</h1>

<div class="container-fluid">
<div class="row">

<div class="col-sm-4">
<h3>Control panel</h3>

<div id="listMovies" class="shiny-html-output"></div>

Title:<input type="text" name="title"><br>

<select name = "genre" class = "form-control">
    <option value="Action">Action</option>
    <option value="Animation">Animation</option>
    <option value="Comedy">Comedy</option>
    <option value="Drama">Drama</option>
    <option value="Documentary">Documentary</option>
    <option value="Romance">Romance</option>
    <option value="Short">Short</option>
</select>

</div>
```

Firstly, we mentioned the heading for the page in the h1 tag. Moving forward, we will be creating our first input, which is the list of movies in the application. It is unusual input, as the output is dynamically rendered. This input is assigned to the `shiny-html-output` class, which refers to the function that renders the UI dynamically. To help you out here, the UI definition can be wrapped in the rendered UI on the server side and then rendered on the UI side, allowing the user interface element to change in response to the user input. The following code block shows the function used in the `server.r` file:

```
output$listMovies = renderUI({

selectInput("pickMovie", "Pick a movie",
choices = moviesSubset() %>%
```

```
sample_n(10) %>%
select(title)
    )
})
```

Next, we will be creating the text control that is given the name title:

```
Title:<input type="text" name="title"><br>
```

This name is then referred to `input$title` on the server side. Next, we will be creating the combo box and giving it the name `genre`, which is also referred to `input$genre` on the server side:

```
<select name = "genre" class = "form-control">
    <option value="Action">Action</option>
    <option value="Animation">Animation</option>
    <option value="Comedy">Comedy</option>
    <option value="Drama">Drama</option>
    <option value="Documentary">Documentary</option>
    <option value="Romance">Romance</option>
    <option value="Short">Short</option>
</select>
```

We can use standard HTML input in Shiny as well. The output is handled using the `div` tag, which is assigned an ID and is referred to as a function in the `server.r` file. For example, we have assigned `budgetYear` as an ID to the `div` tag and class as `shiny-plot-output`, along with information about the `width` and `height`, which tells Shiny it is a plot and what its size is:

```
<div id="budgetYear" class="shiny-plot-output" style="width: 100%; height:
400px"></div>
```

The next few HTML lines show equivalents of the links, text formatting, and code block tag examples that we defined previously using Shiny commands:

```
<p>For more information about <strong>Shiny</strong> look at the
<a href="http://shiny.rstudio.com/articles/">documentation.</a>
</p>
<hr>
<p>If you wish to write some code you may like to use the pre() function
like this:</p>
<pre>sliderInput("year", "Year", min = 1893, max = 2005, value = c(1945,
2005), sep = "")</pre>
```

Next, we will have Shiny HTML output. It is similar to the previous Shiny output we created earlier, but this time we use this output to render a table:

```
<div id = "moviePicker" class = "shiny-html-output"></div>
```

This creates the output we required at the start of the section. Isn't it easy to create an application using HTML?

Adding HTML using the tag() function

Shiny provides a helper function to use basic HTML tags to create your application. However, if there are some HTML tags that are not included in the function, we can use the `tag` function. To find out about the `tag` function, you can simply type names (`tags`) in the console. This will give you all the functions that are available, as seen in the following screenshot:

```
                          Names(tags)

"a" "abbr" "address" "area" "article" "aside" "audio"

"b" "base" "bdi" "bdo" "blockquote" "body" "br" "button"

"canvas" "caption" "cite" "code" "col" "colgroup" "command"

"data" "datalist" "dd" "del" "details" "dfn" "div" "dl" "dt"

"em" "embed" "eventsource"

"fieldset" "figcaption" "figure" "footer" "form"

"h1" "h2" "h3" "h4" "h5" "h6" "head" "header" "hgroup"
```

To use the function, we can simply use `tags$name`, where the name is the function required. The `name` argument becomes the argument within the HTML tag. As you can see in the following screenshot, the first example, `tags$script`, will yield an output of the script `html` tag followed by the named argument `type`. The arguments that do not have names are used as the body of the tag. As seen in the second example, the named argument becomes `href`, whereas the unamed argument, `This is an example`, becomes the body of the HTML tag:

```
                  Using the tags() Function

tags$script(src = "shared/jquery.js", type = "text/javascript")

Output

<script src="shared/jquery.js" type="text/javascript"></script>

tags$a(href="www.example.com", "This is an example")

Output

<a href="www.example.com">This is an example</a>
```

As seen in the previous example, the unnamed arguments are used as the body of the tags. We can use this to nest tags. Let's consider the following example:

```
                              Nesting

tags$head(
  tags$title("HTML movies application"),
  tags$script(src = "shared/jquery.js", type = "text/javascript"),
  tags$script(src = "shared/shiny.js", type = "text/javascript"),
  tags$link(rel="stylesheet", type="text/css",
  href="shared/shiny.css"),
)
```

Here, we are using `tags$head` and we are using a series of other tags separated by commas. In the example, we are using the links that we added at the beginning of the HTML Shiny UI definition that we created in the previous section. The output is the following HTML with the `title`, `scripts`, and style sheet all nested within the `head` section:

```
                        Nesting(continue)
Output
<head>
<title>HTML movies application</title>
<script src="shared/jquery.js" type="text/javascript"></script>
<script src="shared/shiny.js" type="text/javascript"></script>
<link rel="stylesheet" type="text/css" href="shared/shiny.css"/>
</head>
```

There may be some arguments that contain characters that can affect the output in R. In such cases, we will use backticks (`) around the text.

Using CSS

We are done with the basics of the HTML tags and now we will be changing the styles of the application using CSS and a stylesheet. The following screenshot shows the final output that we will be creating using CSS and a style sheet:

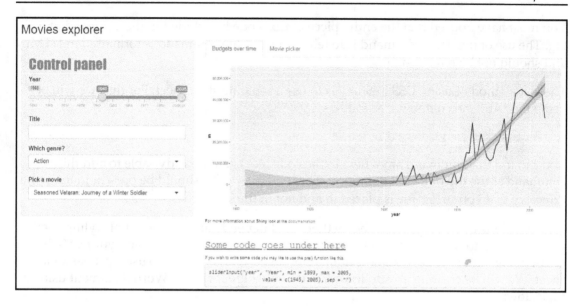

If you have noticed, the font and color of the title of the UI panel, paragraph text size, and formatting of the subheading has changed as compared to the previous application that we used in the *Creating a UI using HTML* section. Let's get started.

The best way to include CSS is by inserting the style with the element that you require. For example, for the heading style in the **Control panel**, we have the h1 tag defined inline with the following tag:

```
h1("Control panel", style = "color:red; font-family:Impact, Charcoal, sans-
serif;")
```

When using CSS in Shiny, basic CSS rules are applied; for example, a semicolon (;) is used to separate elements. The next method for using CSS is to include it in the head section using the tags command:

```
tags$head(
tags$style(HTML("h3 {
color: blue;font-family:courier;
text-decoration: underline;
                        }"
    ))
  )
```

You must have noticed that the entire piece of CSS code is included in the `head` and `style` tag. The use of the `HTML` command is to tell Shiny that the command is formatted in HTML and should not be rendered.

The last method of using CSS in Shiny is to use a separate style sheet. For this, we will be using the `include` command, as follows:

```
includeCSS("styles.css")
```

You can use this command anywhere in the code block, but it is advisable to add this command at the top of the UI definition. The `style.css` file should be present in the same directory that your `ui.r` file is placed in and not in the `www` folder.

Writing CSS is quite simple, but the method used depends on the amount of styling used aligned to the application. Your choice depends on where you want to add your CSS. If you are defining a lot of code in a line a number of times, it is advisable to use a proper style sheet. We will be creating an application to download reports in a Word document using R Markdown.

Dynamic downloadable reports in Shiny

In this section, we will learn how to use the Shiny `downloadhandler` function to render and download reports. We will also learn how to write an R Markdown document and make it dynamic.

Before we begin, let's understand the application that we are going to create. The following screenshot shows the main page of the application, where we have a textbox to change the title of the report and and a button to download the document in a Word file:

On downloading the report, you should find the new title of the document as well as the title of the graph, which are the same as we used in the textbox, as seen in the following screenshot:

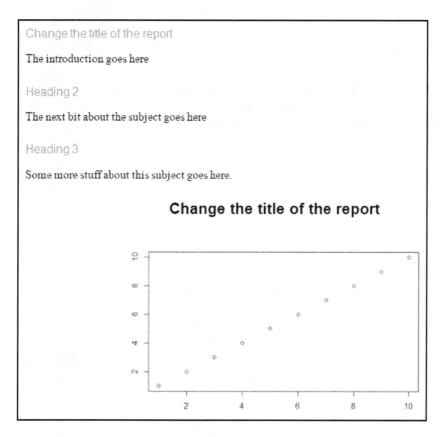

 If you are using a Linux or Ubuntu system, you can open the document using the LibreOffice application found at www.libreoffice.org.

Add the following code to the `ui.r` file in the `DownloadWord` folder:

```
fluidPage(
    titlePanel("Title the report")
    textInput("title", "Title", value = "Your title here"),
    hr(),
    downloadButton("downloadwrodreport", "Download word report")
)
```

The previous code is self-explanatory. It consists of the title of the page, a textbox to add the title to the report's horizontal line, and a button. This button is defined as a **Download** button function that will download the file that is mentioned in our `server.r` file under the `downloadhandler` function.

In the `downloadWord.r` file, we have a library, `rmarkdown`, which is used to make the document rendering function work. The `downloadwordReport` function that we just saw in our `ui.r` file contains the `downlaodHandler` function:

```
library(rmarkdown)
function(input, output){
    output$downloadWordReport =
        downloadHandler(filename = "report.docx",
                    content = function(file){

                        render("report.Rmd", output_format =
"word_document",
                            output_file = file,
                            quiet = TRUE)
            })
    }
```

The `downloadHandler` function has the following structure. The first part will define the filename that is assigned to the report. This filename can be in any form. For example, we can use today's date to provide the filename or any random name with an extension. As you can see in the code, we have simply used `report.docx` in our example. The second part, the `content` function, is defined to write the content using the argument `file` function. This function takes the argument `file` and writes whatever you want to that file using the previously defined `filename`.

In our application, this content will write the content present in the `report.rmd` document into a Word document and assign the filename of `report.docx`, which will be provided to you to download with the changes required.

Now, let's look at the R Markdown document:

```
---
output: word_document
---

# `r input$title`

The introduction goes here

## Heading 2

The next bit about the subject goes here

### Heading 3

Some more stuff about this subject goes here.

```{r, echo = FALSE}

plot(1:10, main = input$title)

```
```

In the Markdown document, first we will mention the output format. This is an optional step as we have already mentioned the output format in the function. We need to be careful when writing the remaining code. This is similar to Markdown document. In the previous code block, you will find various headings that are defined using hashes (#) for headings and subheadings. We have also defined a few inline R functions and code blocks using backticks and curly brackets { }, similar to the method we saw earlier. And finally, there is the plot with the title dynamically taken from the textbox in the UI. We have finally done with creating an application using HTML and CSS. We will now learn how to use HTML templates with R and Shiny.

Using HTML templates

HTML templates are ready-to-use templates combining HTML and Shiny code together in the same code files. In this section, we will learn about a method to include R code written directly to an HTML template and how to use the R code in a separate file reference from the template.

Here, we will create the first application that contains the range slider. Creating a slider using vanilla Shiny code is much easier than using raw HTML:

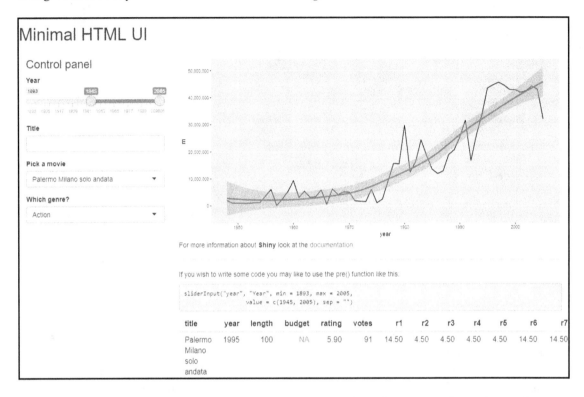

In general, there are two ways of using the HTML template. One way is by using an R function defined inline to the template and the other is by referring an R function to the variables defined in a separate file. In both methods, we will need the three separate `server.r`, `ui.r`, and `.html` files. You can name the HTML file as you like. For demonstration purposes, we have used `template.html`. We can even name the HTML file `apps.html`. The HTML file needs to be placed at the same level as the `server.r` and `ui.r` files and not in a `www` folder.

Here, the `server` file will be similar to the one we created earlier and the `ui.r` file will contain the following line:

```
htmlTemplate("template.html")
```

The preceding line just informs the Shiny app that we will be using the HTML template. Now let's understand what the HTML file contains:

```
<html>
  <head>
    {{ headContent() }}
    {{ bootstrapLib() }}
  </head>
  <body>
    <h1>Minimal HTML UI</h1>
    <div class="container-fluid">
      <div class="row">
        <div class="col-sm-4">
          <h3>Control panel</h3>
            {{ sliderInput("year", "Year", min = 1893, max = 2005, value =
c(1945, 2005), sep = "") }}
            {{ textInput("title", "Title") }}
            <div id="listMovies" class="shiny-html-output"></div>
            {{ selectInput("genre", "Which genre?", c("Action",
"Animation", "Comedy", "Drama", "Documentary", "Romance", "Short")) }}
        </div>
        <div class="col-sm-8">
          {{ plotOutput("budgetYear") }}
          <p>For more information about <strong>Shiny</strong> look at the
          <a
href="http://shiny.rstudio.com/articles/">documentation.</a></p>
          <hr>
          <p>If you wish to write some code you may like to use the pre()
function like this:</p>
          <pre>sliderInput("year", "Year", min = 1893, max = 2005,
              value = c(1945, 2005), sep = "")</pre>

          <div id = "moviePicker" class = "shiny-html-output"></div>
        </div>
      </div>
    </div>
  </body>
</html>
```

The previous HTML code is similar to the raw definition that we used earlier, except for the controls and output. The controls and output are Shiny code instead of HTML code. We can also combine Shiny and HTML to define the controls and output. Let's look at the functions of the Shiny code. At the beginning, in the `head` section, we have two functions; one is `{{ headContent() }}` and the other is `{{ bootstrapLib() }}`.

The head content, `{{ headContent() }}`, will produce the boilerplate HTML that we saw in the previous example about adding the links of JavaScript and CSS. `{{ bootstrapLib() }}` is required to load the Bootstrap library.

You must have noticed that we have defined the slider, textbox, and genre input using the Shiny commands within the HTML file (`template.html`), as seen in the following code block:

```
{{ sliderInput("year", "Year", min = 1893, max = 2005, value = c(1945,
2005), sep = "") }}
{{ textInput("title", "Title") }}
{{ selectInput("genre", "Which genre?", c("Action", "Animation", "Comedy",
"Drama", "Documentary", "Romance", "Short")) }}
```

All these Shiny commands are wrapped in double curly brackets `{{ }}`, similar to the function defined in the `header` section. We are done with the HTML changes. This is the simplest method to add pre-existing HTML frameworks to a Shiny application without using a lot of HTML code blocks and defining the controls. One disadvantage to this method is that we will not be able to use line breaks, as they will not be processed as required.

Let's look at the other method for using the HTML template, where the file structure is similar to the first method of having three files: `server.r`, `ui.r`, and an `.html` file (`template.html`). Here, we will create the HTML file first, which will have the following lines of code:

```
<html>
  <head>
    {{ headContent() }}
    {{ bootstrapLib() }}
  </head>
  <body>
    <h1>Minimal HTML UI</h1>
    <div class="container-fluid">
      <div class="row">
        <div class="col-sm-4">
          <h3>Control panel</h3>
          {{ slider }}
          {{ text }}
        <div id="listMovies" class="shiny-html-output"></div>
          {{ comboBox }}
        </div>
        <div class="col-sm-8">
          {{ thePlot }}
          <p>For more information about <strong>Shiny</strong> look at the
<a href="http://shiny.rstudio.com/articles/">documentation.</a></p>
```

```
            <hr>   <p>If you wish to write some code you may like to
            use the pre() function like this:</p>
            <pre>sliderInput("year", "Year", min = 1893, max = 2005,
                   value = c(1945, 2005), sep = "")</pre>
         <div id = "moviePicker" class = "shiny-html-output"></div>
         </div>
       </div>
     </div>
   </body>
</html>
```

We have here the two standard functions at the top, and the main difference is that we have defined the variable names in place of curly brackets as compared to defining the function inline, as in the previous method. We have defined the `{{ slider }}`, `{{ text }}`, `{{ comboBox }}`, and `{{ thePlot }}` variables for the slider, text input, genre, and the plot, respectively.

You can find the following code files in the `Simple Template 2` folder.

Now it's time to create the `ui.r` file. First, we will define the name of the HTML template and also define the variables used in the HTML file. Your final `ui.r` will look similar to the following structure:

```
htmlTemplate(
  "template.html",
  slider = sliderInput("year", "Year", min = 1893, max = 2005,
                       value = c(1945, 2005), sep = ""),
  text = textInput("title", "Title"),
  thePlot = plotOutput("budgetYear"),
  comboBox = selectInput("genre", "Which genre?",
                      c("Action", "Animation", "Comedy", "Drama",
                        "Documentary", "Romance", "Short"))
)
```

Here, we can see that we have defined the `slider` variable as the `sliderInput` function, `text` as the `textInput` function, `theplot` as the `plotOutput` function, and `comboBox` as the `selectInput` function. We can define all the variables and functions here instead of defining them in HTML functions. For example, you can also define a string that prints the author name that can be used throughout the function. If the name of the author needs to be changed, then we only need to alter one variable rather than changing all the functions throughout.

You can find more information about HTML templates at
`shiny.rstudio.com/articles/templates.html`.

Summary

In this chapter, we learned about the basics of Shiny applications and the use of Shiny commands. We also learned about how to create and style an application using the HTML tags and CSS, and create a downloadable application using the R Markdown document. Later, we covered the use of HTML templates and the use of Shiny and HTML to create dynamic applications. In the next chapter, we'll be looking at Shiny layout functions.

Layout Functions in Shiny 2

In the first chapter, we got introduced to the basics of Shiny applications and the various Shiny commands. The layout functions in Shiny describe the different functions that is available in order to review the applications with each of the layouts with the same content. This chapter explains in detail about producing the different layout functions. We will be covering the following topics throughout the chapter:

- Bootstrap and how it works for Shiny
- How to produce layouts using rows and columns
- The different layout functions available with Shiny
- Navigation bar and navigation list layouts
- Using conditional UI elements, as well as how to take control of the UI

Bootstrap framework

In this section, we will learn about Bootstrap and its framework as well as its usage and the concepts that it brings to web design in the Shiny applications. We will also see how to add a theme to a Bootstrap setup.

Bootstrap is an open source toolkit that makes use of HTML, CSS, and JavaScript. It is of particular interest to web developers because it enables them to make responsive websites that can seamlessly scale up or down depending on the screen it's viewed on, including PC monitors, tablets, and even mobile phones.

Shiny was built on Bootstrap version 3. However, Bootstrap version 4 is available with minor changes. The main content that attracts Shiny developers about Bootstrap is the grid system.

The grid system is a way of organizing content in a sample format, and is initially done by organizing rows and then by columns. Familiarity with Shiny will also breed familiarity with many components of the Bootstrap framework, such as navigation bars, organizing content on a page using a bar with icons and a well panel, which is used to organize inputs and outputs.

 Note that the well panel has been superseded by the card component in version 4.

Modals are another important component; they are popup information boxes that give alerts to your users.

As we move forward and continue to develop with Shiny, it's worth learning about its connections to the Bootstrap framework, so we can easily control content using HTML and CSS. As Shiny is based on the Bootstrap framework, Bootstrap will be inevitably pre-owned whenever Shiny is used.

Moving away from vanilla layout functions, such as a sidebar layout, can be done through Bootstrap. For example, the grid system is the layout of your applications that develop using `fluidPage()` and `fixedPage()`.

Uses of Bootstrap

Bootstrap can be used while moving to HTML templates or raw HTML, although if required, we can use our own CSS. Note that it is worth being aware of the `bootstrapPage()` function, which provides a minimalistic Shiny user interface setup. This function loads the Bootstrap CSS and JavaScript, but doesn't put anything else into HTML. To learn more about the `bootstrapPage()` function, you can visit: `https://shiny.rstudio.com/reference/shiny/1.0.5/bootstrapPage.html`.

Adding themes to Bootstrap

There are many free and open source themes available online if you do not want to use the default theme of Bootstrap.

Using them is as simple as putting the theme inside a `www` folder, which is at the same level as your application, and providing the filename. For example, `sandstone.css` as the theme argument to `fluidPage`, `fixedPage`, `bootstrapPage`, or `navbarPage`.

Producing layout in rows and columns

As we already know, Shiny uses the grid system from Bootstrap to lay out content. There are a couple of ways to carry this out, but built-in Shiny functions are always involved. The differences between the functions are minor and the basic idea of each is the same.

This section will cover the server installation steps of the following functions:

- fluidPage()
- bootstrapPage()
- fixedPage()

fluidPage()

The most standard way of using the grid layout within Shiny is to use the fluidPage() function. The following code snippet illustrates the fluidPage() function:

```
server = function(input, output){

# server code
}
ui = fluidPage(

 fluidRow(
  column(2, wellPanel(p("Column width 2"))),
  column(10, wellPanel(p("Column width 10")))),
   fluidRow(
    column(4, wellPanel(p("Column width 4"))),
    column(4, wellPanel(p("Column width 4"))),
    column(4, wellPanel(p("Column width 4")))))
)
shinyApp(ui = ui, server = server)
```

From the preceding code, the content of this function is organized by rows in which the fluidPage() function wraps the whole interface and adds as many fluid rows that are necessary. In this case, the code shows that the whole interface is composed of two rows.

Rows are made up of columns, and as you can see in the following output, the first row is made up of two columns. One is two units wide and the other is 10 units wide. The number of units should always add up to 12. The next row is made up of three columns, each one four units wide.

There are panels inside the columns so we can see what they are made of and objects such as controls, graphs, tables, and so on are usually put inside them. If we set up the code file with those panels, the Bootstrap framework will take care of the sizing of the elements on whatever browser window we use.

The following screenshot shows the output for the preceding code:

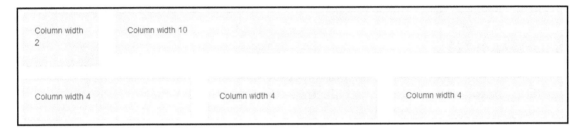

Resizing the window results in a smooth resizing of all the elements, as shown in the following screenshot:

In order to look at nesting columns, use `fluidPage()` as shown in the following code snippet:

```
server = function(input, output){

  # server code
}
ui = fluidPage(

    fluidRow(
     column(2, wellPanel(p("Column width 2"))),
     column(10, wellPanel(p("Column width 10")))),
    fluidRow(
```

```
        column(2, wellPanel(p("Column width 2"))),
        column(10, wellPanel(p("Column width 10"))),
            fluidRow(
                column(6, wellPanel(p("Column width 6"))),
                column(6, wellPanel(p("Column width 6")))
                    )
            )
        )
    )
    shinyApp(ui = ui, server = server)
```

Rows can be nested within columns in order to nest content underneath individual elements. In the preceding code, the last column has a nested row comprising of two columns.

The columns in this new row have widths that add up to 12, even though they are only for a subset of the width of the page. Columns always add up to 12, no matter how much width of the screen they are assigned to. This code will produce two boxes of equal width underneath the column of 10 width, as shown in the following screenshot:

bootstrapPage()

The bootstrapPage() function does not do anything except load the Bootstrap framework.

Once the framework is loaded, the well panel is now unhelpfully overlapping the right-hand side of the screen; however, it does still resize, as shown in the following screenshot:

```
Column width 2




Column width 10




Column width 2




Column width 10




Column width 6




Column width 6
```

Adding a fluid container `div` around the code makes the user interface, and even the HTML that is produced, exactly the same as in the previous `fluidPage()` example, as shown in the code snippet:

```
server = function(input, output){

  # server code
}
ui = bootstrapPage(
    div(class = "container-fluid",

    fluidRow(
        column(2, wellPanel(p("Column width 2"))),
        column(10, wellPanel(p("Column width 10")))),
    fluidRow(
        column(2, wellPanel(p("Column width 2"))),
        column(10, wellPanel(p("Column width 10"))),
            fluidRow(
                column(6, wellPanel(p("Column width 6")))),
```

```
                    column(6, wellPanel(p("Column width 6")))
                        )
                )
            )
        )
    )
    shinyApp(ui = ui, server = server)
```

The output of this application looks identical to the nested columns produced by fluidPage(). The HTML that is cogenerated is also the same.

fixedPage()

The use of the fixedPage() function gives different results as compared to the fluidPage() and bootstrapPage() functions.

fixedPage() should be used with fixed rows, as shown in the following code snippet example:

```
server = function(input, output){

 # server code
}
ui = fixedPage(

    fixedRow(
        column(2, wellPanel(p("Column width 2"))),
        column(8, wellPanel(p("Column width 8")), offset = 2))
)
shinyApp(ui = ui, server = server)
```

When we look at the final application, we can see that a gap has been added, as shown in the following screenshot, which is achieved by using the offset command:

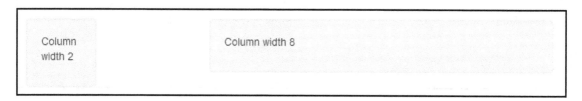

We can also see that, although it is automatically resized, as with the fluid row, the resizing takes up space with little jumps, as with the fixed row example.

Here, the `offset` command has been added as an argument to the column.

Navigation bar and the navigation list based layout

Shiny allows you to layout your application using `navbars` and `navlists`. These are layouts that come from the Bootstrap framework. However, `navlist` has disappeared as a named class in Bootstrap 3.

Navbar panel application

From the following screenshot, in the first tab (**Budgets over time**), we have the year, title, and genre controls, as well as the graph underneath containing content from the **Movies explorer** application:

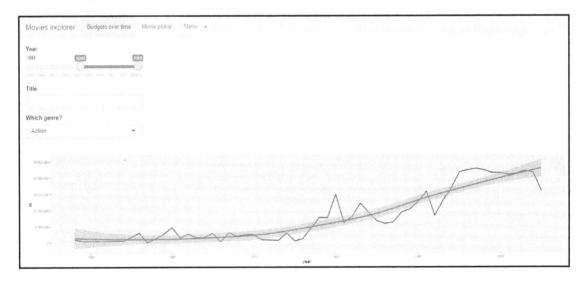

Budget over time tab

On the next tab (**Movie picker**), we have a table with the movie selector combo box. The `navbar` layout gives you buttons along the top, which allows you to select different tab panels, as shown in the following screenshot:

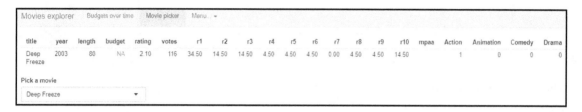

Movie picker

As there is no sidebar here, the controls are given with the associated output, as shown in the following screenshot:

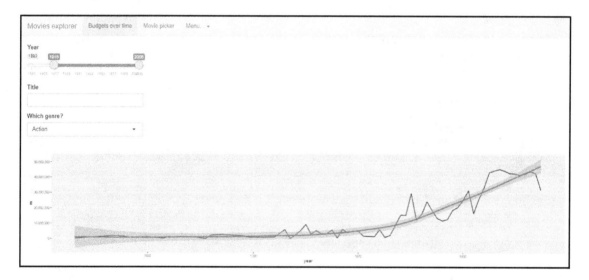

Finally, there is a **Menu** tab, which demonstrates the nesting that is possible on a **Menu** button. This button includes two controls, both of which lead to a tab panel including links to the **About** section and the **Reference** section, as shown in the following screenshot:

Menu tab

The following screenshot illustrates the information of the **About** section:

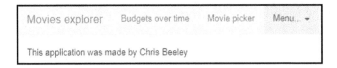

About tab

The information in the **Reference** section is as follows:

Reference tab

Of course in the full application, these controls can point to reactive outputs, such as graphs and tables, or even longer pieces of text that give you more detail about the application. The code snippet for this is as follows:

```
navbarPage("Movies explorer",
           id = "navBar",
           tabPanel(
             "Budgets over time", value = "graph",
             sliderInput("year", "Year", min = 1893, max = 2005,
                         value = c(1945, 2005), sep = ""),
             textInput("title", "Title"),
             selectInput("genre", "Which genre?",
                         c("Action", "Animation", "Comedy", "Drama",
                           "Documentary", "Romance", "Short")),
             plotOutput("budgetYear", height = "300px")),
           tabPanel(
             "Movie picker", value = "table",
             tableOutput("moviePicker"),
             uiOutput("listMovies")),
           navbarMenu("Menu...",
             tabPanel("About", value = "about",
                 p("This application was made
                         by Chris Beeley")),
             tabPanel("Reference", value = "reference",
                 p("For more details see ",
    a("https://shiny.rstudio.com/reference/shiny/latest/navbarPage.html"))
  )
        )
  )
```

Instead of being set up with `fluidPage()`, `navbarPage` is set up, unsurprisingly, with the `navbarPage` function. We have assigned an ID as well, which is an option which can be accessed using `input$id`. For example, in our application, we will be using `input$navbar`. This will allow the application to return the value of the current isolated tab.

As can be seen in this application, the input `navbar` takes the value of the graph, the table, **About** or **Reference**, depending on which tab is selected. Multiple tab panels can be selected from one control with a dropdown, as seen in the application earlier. For example, in our application, we have used `navbarMenu` to wrap several `tabPanels`, having assigned each title a value for the user to select the desired tab.

 Note that the `navbar` menu is also used to wrap several tab panels, both the title and the value, which allows the user to set their desired tab from a drop-down menu.

NavlistPanel application

Here, we will be creating an application using the `navlistPanel` application. This is a similar application including the content from the `ggplot2` movies dataset. Here however, `tabPanels` is selected from a menu on the side, where we see the controls and a port with the output on the tab panel. You define the application in `server.r` the file.

The first tab (**Budgets over time**) will lead you to the graph with the year, title, and genre:

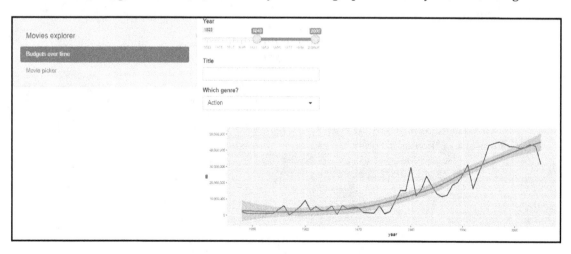

Budget over time using navlistPanel

The second tab (**Movie picker**) will lead you to the movie selector, as shown in the following screenshot:

Movie picker using navlistPanel

From the following code snippet, unlike `navbar`, `navlistPanel` is added to a page set up with `fluidPage()`. Here, we have a title and an ID so the currently selected tab can be accessed using `input$id`, which in this case is `input$navlist`.

Having set up the list, add tab panels, each one with a title and a value, which can be accessed using `input$navlist`, as seen in the following code snippet:

```
fluidPage(

    navlistPanel(
        "Movies explorer", id = "navList",

    tabPanel(
        "Budgets over time", value = "graph",
        sliderInput("year", "Year", min = 1893, max = 2005,
                    value = c(1945, 2005), sep = ""),
        textInput("title", "Title"),
        selectInput("genre", "Which genre?",
                    c("Action", "Animation", "Comedy", "Drama",
                    "Documentary", "Romance", "Short")),
        plotOutput("budgetYear", height = "300px")),
    tabPanel("Movie picker", value = "table",
             tableOutput("moviePicker"),
             uiOutput("listMovies"))
    )
)
```

Summary of layout functions

In this section, we will look at all of the layout functions to give an overview of what is available. We will review applications with each of the layouts with the same content to give an idea of how they all compare.

flowlayout

The following screenshot illustrates the `flowlayout` function of the setup. Elements are ordered left to right and top to bottom, as seen in the following screenshot:

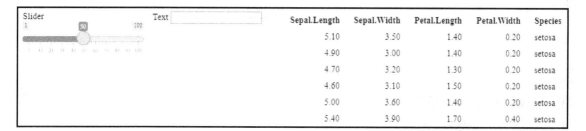

flowlayout

Resizing the application window causes the elements to reorder themselves so that they fit left to right and top to bottom.

sidebarlayout

The most common `sidebarlayout` setup features inputs on the left-hand side and outputs can be found on right-hand side of the screen, as shown in the following screenshot:

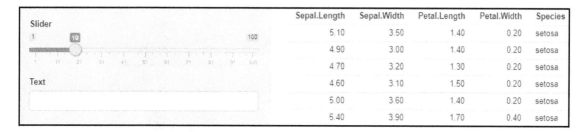

sidebarlayout

splitlayout

`splitlayout` takes as many elements as you give it and arranges them on the page left to right. By default, each column is given the same width but they can be adjusted manually, as shown in the following screenshot:

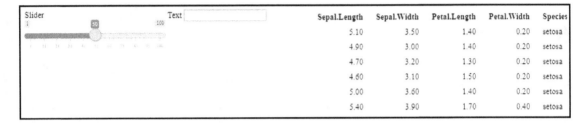

splitlayout

verticallayout

The following screenshot illustrates `verticallayout`, which, as the name suggests, arranges elements vertically:

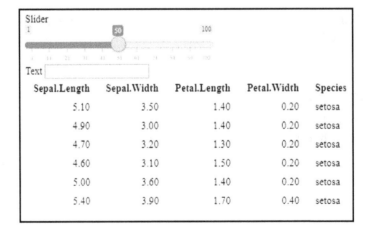

Vertical flow layout

fluidrow

The following screenshot illustrates the `fluidrow` function. When used with columns, fluid rows can be used to lay out your application flexibly:

	Sepal.Length	Sepal.Width	Petal.Length	Petal.Width	Species
	5.10	3.50	1.40	0.20	setosa
	4.90	3.00	1.40	0.20	setosa
	4.70	3.20	1.30	0.20	setosa
	4.60	3.10	1.50	0.20	setosa
	5.00	3.60	1.40	0.20	setosa
	5.40	3.90	1.70	0.40	setosa

fluidrow layout

navbar and navlist

The `navbar` function creates icons at the top that lead to navigation table tab panels. The `navlist` creates links at the side of a page that allow you to do the same thing. Both of these setups will resize themselves as the browser window itself does, as long as the default value of fluid set to `TRUE`.

In our example, the server code has been kept constant throughout and it returns a table. The first function we looked at was `flowlayout`, which orders elements from left to right and from top to bottom. The code is very simple (as it's just flow layout), as shown in the code snippet:

```
server = function(input, output) {

    output$table = renderTable({

        head(iris)
    })
}
ui = flowLayout(
    sliderInput("slider", "Slider", min = 1, max = 100, value = 50),
    textInput("text", "Text"),
    tableOutput("table")
)
shinyApp(ui, server)
```

The sidebar layout is often seen in vanilla Shiny applications. To use one ourselves, we need to use `fluidPage` to set up the page, and then the `sidebarLayout` function followed by the two components, the sidebar panel, and the main panel. These can contain as many elements as you like, as shown in the following code snippet:

```
server = function(input, output) {
  output$table = renderTable({
    head(iris)
  })
}

ui = fluidPage(
  sidebarLayout(
    sidebarPanel(
      sliderInput("slider", "Slider", min = 1, max = 100, value = 50),
      textInput("text", "Text")),
    mainPanel(tableOutput("table"))
  )
)
  shinyApp(ui, server)
```

The `splitlayout` function is very simple, and it does not require a call to `fluidPage()`. In the code snippet, we can see that specified widths (in a percentage format) tell Shiny how much width is needed for each cell from the following code:

```
server = function(input, output) {
  output$table = renderTable({
    head(iris)
  })
}
ui = splitLayout(
  cellWidths = c("20%", "20%", "60%"),
  sliderInput("slider", "Slider", min = 1, max = 100, value = 50),
  textInput("text", "Text"),
  tableOutput("table")
)
shinyApp(ui, server)
```

The vertical layer has a very similar structure; it's only each component within the code to vertical layout, as shown in the following code example:

```
server = function(input, output) {
  output$table = renderTable({
    head(iris)
  })
}
ui = verticalLayout(
```

```
        sliderInput ("slider", "Slider", min = 1, max = 100, value = 50),
        textInput ("text", "Text"),
        tableOutput ("table")
    )
    shinyApp (ui, server)
```

The `fluidPage` function is composed of fluid rows, which are themselves composed of columns that are each given a width adding up to 12 in each row.

In this example, we only use one row, but in a more complex application we are free to add more, as shown in the following code snippet:

```
server = function (input, output) {
    output$table = renderTable ({
        head (iris)
    })
}
ui = fluidPage (
    fluidRow (
        column (width = 4,
                sliderInput ("slider", "Slider", min = 1, max = 100, value = 50),
                textInput ("text", "Text")),
        column (width = 8,
                tableOutput ("table")
            )
        )
    )
shinyApp (ui, server)
```

As we saw earlier, a `navbar` is set up by using `navbarPage ()`, which gives the page a name and a set of tab panels, each of which is also given a name, as shown in the following code snippet:

```
server = function (input, output) {
    output$table = renderTable ({
        head (iris)
    })
}
ui = navbarPage ("Movies explorer",
                 tabPanel ("Inputs",
                        sliderInput ("slider", "Slider",
                                    min = 1, max = 100, value = 50),
                        textInput ("text", "Text")),
                 tabPanel ("Table", tableOutput ("table"))
)

shinyApp (ui, server)
```

`navlist` is very similar, except in this case it is necessary to call `fluidPage` first.

Conditional UI

Shiny provides a lots of ways to make the user experience as simple and easy as possible. By controlling what the user sees, taking control of the user's inputs, and giving the user feedback about what the application is doing and why, it is possible to make the experience easy to follow for everyone.

So, in this section, we will look at the following topics:

- Using the conditional UI function
- Controlling the user interface with `observe()`
- Using modals to give messages to the user

The first thing to note here is that the movie selector does not show on the graph screen, as shown in the following screenshot:

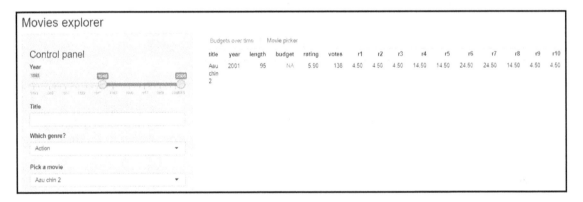

Conditional UI function under Movie picker tab

It is often useful in a large application to show the user only those controls that can currently be used. This prevents your UI from being cluttered and helps show how the application works.

As you can see in the following screenshot, the **Control panel** appears as well as a decent graph that shows the user a sensible time span of budgets:

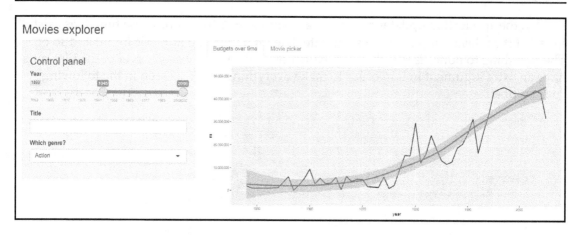

Budgets over time tab with graph

If the year span that the user chooses is less than 10 years, the control is reset. This stops users from generating a short graph with very little information in it. It is important that this is communicated to the user, and can be achieved using a modal popup, as shown in the following screenshot:

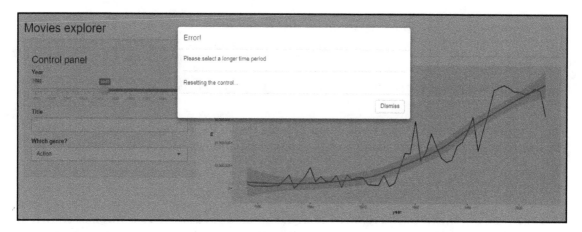

There are two functions available for displaying a modal popup dialog, in which one is for creating and the other for showing. For our purposes, we will just create a simple dialog with modalDialog and then display it using showModal.

As you can see in the following code snippet, the modalDialog accepts Shiny elements, such as strings and a horizontal rule, and the box can also be given to Tyco. There are more options available relating to the size of the box, but that's not important at the moment.

Finally, the application updates the `updatessliderInput` function. These functions exist for all of the relevant inputs, such as update date input, update numeric input, and so on. The first thing to notice is that the call to function at the top of every server of the files must have an extra argument in it in order to make everything work, as seen in the following code snippet:

```
    movies %>% filter(year %in% seq(input$year[1], input$year[2]),
                      UQ(sym(input$genre)) == 1)
})

  observe({
      if(input$year[2] - input$year[1] <= 10){

          showModal(modalDialog(
          title = "Error!",
          "Please select a longer time period", hr(), "Resetting the
control..."
          ))

          updateSliderInput(session, "year", value = c(1945, 2005))
      }
})

  output$budgetYear = renderPlot({
      budgetByYear = summarise(group_by(moviesSubset(), year),
                               m = mean(budget, na.rm = TRUE))

  ggplot(budgetByYear[complete.cases(budgetByYear), ],
  ...
```

This is true for a few Shiny functions, including the one in the following example. As we can see in the snippet, we are using an `input`, `output`, and `session` within the `function` call:

```
function(input, output, session)
```

This `session` argument can be referred to in the `updateSliderInput` control, as shown in the following code snippet, where we have edited the `year`. Here, we can change features such as the range, step size, the value, the label, and so on:

```
updateSliderInput(session, "year", value = c(1945, 2005))
```

Summary

In this chapter, we looked at the Bootstrap framework and how Shiny makes use of it, and how to build an application layout using rows and columns. We explored the navigation bar, navigation list—based layouts, and also looked at an overview of all of the layout functions. Lastly, we looked at using conditional UI elements and how to control the UI.

In the next chapter, we will be taking a look at dashboards and how to put together our very first dashboard.

3
Dashboards

In this chapter, we're going to take a look at the following topics:

- Building your first dashboard
- Laying out a dashboard
- The use of icons
- Producing notifications, messages, and tasks on your dashboard
- The use of info boxes
- Adding Google Charts

Building your first dashboard

In this section, we will look at putting together your first dashboard. We will cover the code structure for a Shiny dashboard, and we will also look at putting together a simple example.

To make a Shiny dashboard, you will need to download the package using the `install.packages` command. Note that the package is then loaded in the preamble of the UI to our file.

There are two methods of structuring the code file for a Shiny dashboard and it also requires the setup of three components: `dashboardHeader`, `dashboardSidebar`, and `dashboardBody`. Using the first method, these three components can be passed to `dashboardPage` very simply, as shown here:

```
dashboardPage(
   dashboardHeader(),
   dashboardSidebar(),
   dashboardBody(),
)
```

Using the second method, header, sidebar, and body can all be set up separately and then passed to dashboardPage, as shown here:

```
header = dashboardHeader()
sidebar = dashboardSidebar()
body = dashboardBody()
dashboardPage(header, sidebar, body)
```

I would strongly advise always using the second method in any decent-sized application, because it simplifies the code structure, but you may have your own preference on this matter. If you feel the other method is better, you can write the code in that way.

Let's have a look at the application. As you can see in the following screenshot, this is the **Movies explorer** application we've been using throughout this book, but rewritten as a dashboard:

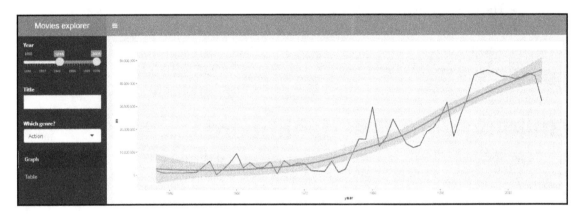

You can see the header at the top left, with a title, the controls over on the left, and the output on the right. So far, it looks like a standard sidebar layout, showing the application. As we work through this chapter, we will add more and more stuff to make it really powerful and attractive.

The server.R code file is the same as it has been throughout when we've used this application, and we will not go into it now. As we already mentioned in the previous chapters, the ui.R file loads the shinydashboard package, as shown here:

```
library(shinydashboard)
```

The header is easily defined using the title argument to give the application a title:

```
header = dashboardHeader(title = "Movies explorer")
```

The width of the title can also be set, and it is also possible to turn off the header completely. You can type `?dashboardHeader` into the console for more information. The sidebar is very easily set up, just as a sidebar in a sidebar layout application, with inputs listed within the `dashboardSidebar` function:

```
sidebar = dashboardSidebar(
  sliderInput("year", "Year", min = 1893, max = 2005,
              value = c(1945, 2005), sep = ""),
  textInput("title", "Title"),
  selectInput("genre", "Which genre?",
              c("Action", "Animation", "Comedy", "Drama",
                "Documentary", "Romance", "Short")),

  sidebarMenu(
    menuItem("Graph", tabName = "graph"),
    menuItem("Table", tabName = "table")
  )
)
```

A tab-like output is achieved using the `sidebarMenu` function, which creates buttons within the sidebar, and these can be used to select different outputs. In the preceding code example, we use the `sidebarMenu` function and then, within it, set up individual buttons with `menuItem`. Each is given a label and a name. And this is the name that we referred to in the body of the dashboard, to determine which output is selected by which button. Now, for some types of dashboard design, no inputs will be included on the sidebar, and they will all be placed in the dashboard body with the outputs. This is not done in this case, partly because of the way the application works, but also to demonstrate both methods for placing inputs, on the sidebar and in the body.

The body is set up, with tab items wrapping individual tab item functions. Tab names are taken from the names we already set up in the sidebar. You can see `graph` and `table`, referring to the tab names already set up within the sidebar in the following code example:

```
body = dashboardBody(
  tabItems(
    tabItem(tabName = "graph",
            plotOutput("budgetYear")
    ),
    tabItem(tabName = "table",
            tableOutput("moviePicker"),
            uiOutput("listMovies")
    )
  )
)
```

We then give the relevant output within each time item. We have the `graph` in the first tab, and the `table` in the second tab. After defining our `header`, `sidebar`, and `body`, we now use `dashboardPage` to put them all together:

```
dashboardPage(header, sidebar, body)
```

Laying out a dashboard

In this section, we will look at how to make your application attractive and well laid out using boxes and the `fluidRow()` function. We will take out the sidebar menu buttons that we used in the previous section to switch between different pages in the dashboard, and lay everything out on one page. Also, we will look at the use of tabbed boxes, for when you want one box to contain several pieces of content.

Let's look at the application here. We've upgraded the table to a data table using the `DT` package, because it can be made to scale better on the page. To pick the movie, it's displayed right next to the table, and the graph and year selector are below it, as shown in the following screenshot:

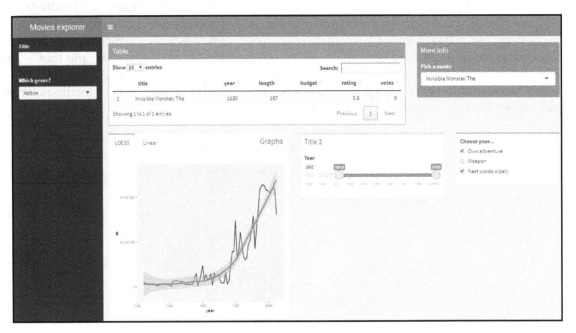

A dummy control is placed next to the real control to give a better example of how to lay out multiple elements, and how they look. The movies selector can be collapsed, and there are tabs on the graph box. One gives a plot fitted with the lowest curve, which bends with the trend in the data, and the other gives a linear trend, which is just a straight line.

The first thing to know is that we've loaded the DT package in both the server.R and ui.R files. You will need to install it the first time. DT is a package for R that uses the JavaScript data tables package to produce powerful and attractive data tables. For more information, you can refer to *Getting Started with Shiny* by Chris Beeley, published by Packt.

You will also see that in the server.R file, within the renderDataTable function, we've added extensions = "Responsive":

```
output$moviePicker = renderDataTable({
    filter(moviesSubset(), title == input$pickMovie)[, 1:6]
}, extensions = "Responsive")
```

There are several extensions that can be loaded here. This one makes the table responsive; that is to say, it ensures that it scales nicely with the window and the rest of the content. Then the other thing of note in the server.R file is another function to return a graph, this time with a linear trend rather than a lowest trend line. lm stands for linear model, and in the budgetYear plotting function, it's defined as lowest smooth (loess). For more information on line to trend in ggplot, type ?geom_smooth in the console.

If you look at the ui.R file, the sidebar has been simplified and only two controls are placed in it: the title of the graph and one control. Although you can make a dashboard without boxes around the elements, as we did in the previous section, it gives a nice appearance if you place your content on the dashboard in boxes. The boxes themselves are laid out using fluid rows, which we learned about in the previous chapter. And just like when we are using fluid rows, we again specify the width to the box function, specifying numbers that add up to 12.

There are lots of other optional arguments that are used throughout this example to give you an idea of what they do. One of the most useful ones is status, which affects the color of the header of the control. This is something else that's comes from the world of Bootstrap. Info, for example, is blue and success is green. For a full list, type ?validatestatuses into the console. solidHeader gives the header a nice solid background. As opposite to it, it is not selected, when you get the thin line, as in the **Choose your...** checkbox control.

You can also select a background color. For a list, type `?validcolors` in the console. You can also set the width and the height, which is usually expressed in pixels. If you don't select this, it will be as long as it needs to be to contain the content. You can also select whether boxes are collapsible, using the `collapsible = TRUE` argument, then the movie picker control will become collapsible.

So, we've seen how to lay out our content using `fluidRow` and `box`, and some of the arguments that are commonly used to make the interface attractive. The last thing of note in the `ui.R` file is the use of a tabbed box. This is very similar to using tabbed content in a vanilla Shiny application, except we use the `tabBox` function. This is then passed to panels, just like in vanilla Shiny. And just like in vanilla Shiny, we can optionally provide an ID to the panel in order to allow us to return the currently selected tab using an input dollar sign ID. We can provide each tab panel with a title, and optionally, a label to be returned with the input dollar sign ID, together with whatever content we want the box to have. The result looks like this:

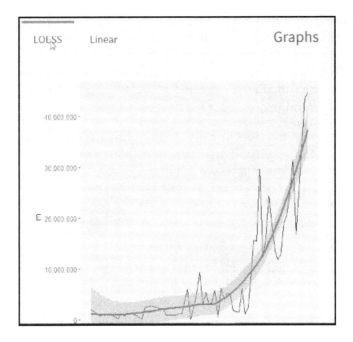

This is a **Linear** and **LOESS** translatable from each tab. Let's look at a column-based layout to better align the UI elements that we were using. Let's look at the application. As you can see in the following screenshot, the graphs have been taken out of the tab box and placed next to each other:

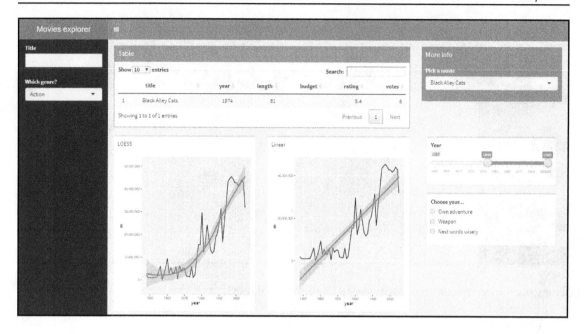

The two controls are now in a column, and together they take up about the same height as the graph, which gives the application a more seamless appearance.

We can see that this effect is achieved very easily by adding both boxes to the last column, and setting the width of each to 12, the maximum width. This causes them to be displayed on top of each other.

Adding icons to your dashboards

In this section, we will add icons to your dashboard, or, in fact, to any Shiny application. We will look at choosing which icon library you want to use, and how to format your icons.

Let's look at an example application. There are three icons in this application. We can see first of all the more standard use of icons here, to select the graph and table:

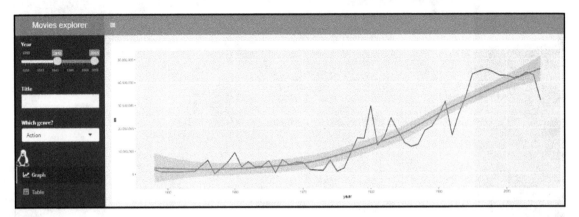

The graph icon is from the Font Awesome library of icons, and the table icon is from the glyphicon set. We can see also enlarge and spin the next penguin, also from the font or a set. This is to show some of the formatting options that are possible.

There are two icon libraries accessible from within Shiny: Font Awesome and glyphicon. For more details on each, visit the following links:

- `https://fontawesome.com/icons?from=io`
- `https://getbootstrap.com/docs/3.3/components/`

Using them is very simple. The Font Awesome library simply uses the `icon` command with the name of the desired icon. The list of available icons is in the first link. To use the cliff icon library, simply add the `live = cliff` argument. The list of cliff icons is available in the second link.

Formatting is simple. The Font Awesome library size can be selected to use the `class` argument, `fa-lg`, which is one-third as large, `fa-2x`, which is twice as big, `fa-3x`, which is three times as big, all the way up to five times as big. Adding spin is as simple as adding a face spin to the argument. Spin and three times size is the code used to make the spinning Linux penguin in the example application.

The Linux penguin is placed in between the UI elements, as can be seen here:

```
icon("linux", class = "fa-spin fa-3x")
```

Adding constant tab buttons is as simple as adding them to the `menuItem` definition function in the `sidebarMenu` definition. Icons can be used anywhere you like. Now we will look at adding them to an application in windows. The application looks like the following; as you can see, there are icons for each of the tabs:

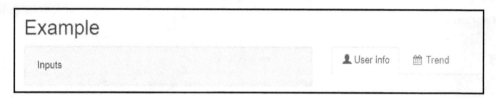

The code is very simple; this is a very simple application written in the single `app.R` file. You can see that the icons are added directly to the tab panels here:

```
tabPanel("User info", icon = icon("user", lib = "glyphicon")),
tabPanel("Trend", icon = icon("calendar"))
```

Adding notifications, messages, and tasks

In this section, we will talk about adding notifications, messages, and tasks, and then how to make the content of them dynamic.

Let's look at the example application. As you can see in the following screenshot, this is a dashboard where we've added icons to the header to allow us access to some menus, tasks, notifications, and messages:

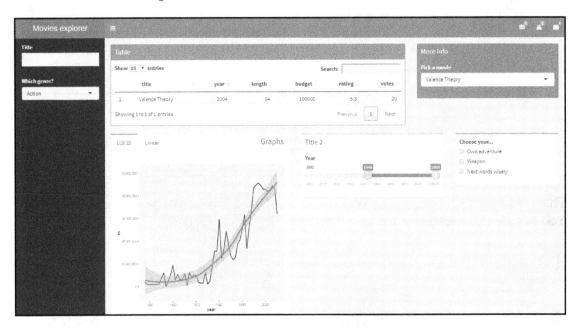

Let's look at the code. In the case where the messages within the menu are static, the code is very simple. The dropdownMenu function is used, to which is added the type, that is, notification message or task, and optionally the status, which affects the color of the little number next to each icon, which gives the number of entries within it. The statuses are the same as the Bootstrap statuses we came across earlier in this chapter. A list is available by typing ?validstatuses in the console. Having performed this setup for tasks, a set of task items is added using the taskItem function. Each sector value is a percentage completion and some text for the name of the task, and the additional collar and hyperlink. This is very simple but it's highly unrealistic. You're very unlikely to make an application that has static values for many of these entries. Perhaps one or two items and notifications might be hardcoded, but everything else is to be rendered on the fly.

Let's look, therefore, at how to render the other two menus, notifications, and messages on the fly. The first difference is on the UI side. We use the dropdownMenuOutput function in the dropdownMenu function. We can see that the name of the control is given to this function. This will be referenced as output dollar sign notifications in the server.R file.

The rest of the processing is done on the `server.R` file. The function that we use to build a menu is `renderMenu`. This will ultimately be passed the output of `dropdownMenu`, which is a function that we already saw in `ui.R`, building the static menu. In turn, this function accepts either the results of the `taskItem` function, the `notificationItem` function, or the `messageItem` function. You can list the elements separated by column, commas but it will often be more convenient and easier to read if we make them into a list first. We can see that in the notifications example here, where we've hardcoded static content into a list of notification items. In a real application, of course, the list will be generated dynamically. `dropdownMenu` can now accept, instead of a comma-separated set of elements, a list using the `.list` argument.

 Note that within a notification menu item, as well as text in the notification, you can add an icon and the status, again based on the Bootstrap status colors.

For the message output, we've added a little bit of dynamic output by randomizing the messages. Again, the individual message items we combined into a list, and this list is passed to `dropdownMenu`. Messages need a message body and information about who they are from, and can optionally be given a different icon. The icon defaults the user and a time or date, which is just a string and can be anything at all (yesterday, 5 minutes ago, the 14th of February, whatever you like). You can see that each of those elements is randomized into a list of two message.

Info boxes and value boxes

In this section, we're going to look at more UI elements that you can use to make your content professional: info boxes and value boxes. In most cases, you will want to make their content dynamic. So, we will look to at how to render them on the server side.

Let's look at the application:

The top row is made up of info boxes. They can be given a color, and this color can be used just in the side panel or throughout, as in the final element on this row. The second row is very similar and it's made up of value boxes. They work much the same way, but they look a little different. As you can see, the bottom row replicates the content of the top row, and the dynamic box reacts in a simple way to the control of the application. The boxes react to the **Which genre?** control, and the blue boxes react to the **Year**. In a real application, of course, you will want to place more interesting information in these controls.

Let's look at the code example:

```
body = dashboardBody(
  fluidRow(
    infoBox("Average budget ($M)", 25, icon = icon("money"), color =
"green")        infoBoxOutput("infoBoxYear"),
```

```
    infoBoxOutput("infoBoxGenre")
  ),
```

As you can see, the info box is a place in a `fluidRow`. The first one that we've defined is just static; it's hardcoded into the interface. It says the average budget in millions of dollars is `25`. The first argument gives the label, and the second, the value. The value is usually a number, but do note that you can put a string in if you prefer. We will do this in one of the later examples. There is also an icon. If you don't provide an icon, the default value of a `graph` will be used, which is not very helpful a lot of the time. It's a good idea to provide a color, unless you want `aqua`, which is the default. Most of the time, you will not want to hardcode the content of these boxes, and then will dynamically use either the user for interface, or the content to a database, values from an API, and so on. Dynamic elements are achieved with notifications, messages, and tasks.

A new function, `infoBoxOutput`, is used on the UI side. And another function, the render info box, is used on the server side. Let's take a look at the server code now. Note that this UI argument references the name of the UI `infoBoxYear`. This will be referred to in the `server.R` file. And we see here the use of `renderInfoBox` on the server side, referencing the name that we just saw on the UI side, `infoBoxYear`. Again, it is provided with a label and value, in this case a string, an icon, and a color:

```
output$infoBoxYear = renderInfoBox({
    infoBox(
        "Years", paste(input$year[1], " to ", input$year[2]),
        icon = icon("calendar-o"),
        color = "blue"
    )
})
```

Info boxes can optionally be filled with the selected color as well, by setting the `fill` parameter type to `TRUE`. The code and principles are very much the same for value boxes. Here is the code for a static value box over on the UI side:

```
fluidRow(
    valueBox("Average budget ($M)", 25, icon = icon("money"), color =
"green"),
    valueBoxOutput("valueBoxYear"),
    valueBoxOutput("valueBoxGenre")
```

Again, we give it a label, value, icon, and color. The dynamic values are created using `valueBoxOutput` here on the UI side, passing, as usual, the name that will be referenced in `server.R`. In the `server.R` file, these elements are produced using `renderValueBox`. Again, it contains a UI base function, `valueBox`, which is, as usual, passed the label, value, icon, and color. Value boxes cannot be given a value for `fill`; they are filled in by default.

Adding Google Charts to your dashboard

In this section, we will look at the different Google Charts that are available, and talk about why you might want to use them. We will see how to add them to a Shiny application. We will also see how to reskin your dashboard to a different color.

Google Charts is a free resource with which you can draw statistical graphics on any web page. They need an internet connection to work, but other than that limitation they're extremely easy to use, perhaps even easier in Shiny using the `googleVis` package. You will need to install this package with `install.packages("googleVis")`. There's a gallery of the different graphics available at

`https://developers.google.com/chart/interactive/docs/gallery`. For our dashboard, we selected the gauge control, which is an attractive addition to the dashboard, and not possible with `besar` or `ggplot`. Although, it is possible in other contributors.

Let's have a look at the application:

As you can see, we've changed the header of the dashboard so, it isn't purple. We've also added a gauge using Google Charts. You can see that it shows the rating of the current isolated movement. And we might have some color to control, 0 to 5 is red, 5 to 7 is yellow, and 7 to 10 is green.

Let's look at the code. The first thing to notice is the argument to recall the header. We simply add `skin = "purple"` to the `dashboardPage` function. Valid colors are blue, black, purple, green, red, and yellow. Let's now look at the Google Charts control. It is very simply on the UI side, with the `htmlOutput` function. This function can be used to add any HTML content to the UI. It is surrounded with a `div` and is marked as HTML.

Let's look at the server side:

```
output$gauge <- renderGvis({
    df = data.frame(Label = "Rating",
                    Value = filter(moviesSubset(),
                                   title == input$pickMovie)[, "rating"])
    gvisGauge(df,
              options = list(min = 0, max = 10, greenFrom = 7,
                             greenTo = 10, yellowFrom = 5, yellowTo = 7,
                             redFrom = 0, redTo = 5))
})
```

The first function to note is `renderGvis`. This is a function that allows you to create these charts using Shiny. Within this function, we will find the function that creates the chart (in this case, `gvisGgage`). This will vary depending on the graph you wish to draw. This particular function accepts a two-column data frame. It doesn't matter what the names of the variables are, but the first should be whatever you want the text on the gauge to read, and the second should be whatever value you want the gauge to have. Multiple row data frames will produce several gauges, but in this case, we've gone with just one. The options are provided in a list and will vary according to the type of graph used. In this case, we've given the minimum and maximum values; otherwise, one of the helpful defaults will be used, as well as the range of scores corresponding to green, yellow, and red.

Summary

In this chapter, we've looked at how to get started with the basic structure of a dashboard, we've looked at how to lay out your dashboard content, and how to add icons, notifications, messages, and tasks. We also looked at adding some polish to your dashboard using info boxes, and then how to take advantage of the library of plots available from Google Charts.

Other Books You May Enjoy

If you enjoyed this book, you may be interested in these other books by Packt:

Data Analysis with R - Second Edition
Tony Fischetti

ISBN: 9781788393720

- Gain a thorough understanding of statistical reasoning and sampling theory
- Employ hypothesis testing to draw inferences from your data
- Learn Bayesian methods for estimating parameters
- Train regression, classification, and time series models
- Handle missing data gracefully using multiple imputation
- Identify and manage problematic data points
- Learn how to scale your analyses to larger data with Rcpp, data.table, dplyr, and parallelization
- Put best practices into effect to make your job easier and facilitate reproducibility

Hands-On Data Visualization with Bokeh
Kevin Jolly

ISBN: 9781789135404

- Installing Bokeh and understanding its key concepts
- Creating plots using glyphs, the fundamental building blocks of Bokeh
- Creating plots using different data structures like NumPy and Pandas
- Using layouts and widgets to visually enhance your plots and add a layer of interactivity
- Building and hosting applications on the Bokeh server
- Creating advanced plots using spatial data

Leave a review - let other readers know what you think

Please share your thoughts on this book with others by leaving a review on the site that you bought it from. If you purchased the book from Amazon, please leave us an honest review on this book's Amazon page. This is vital so that other potential readers can see and use your unbiased opinion to make purchasing decisions, we can understand what our customers think about our products, and our authors can see your feedback on the title that they have worked with Packt to create. It will only take a few minutes of your time, but is valuable to other potential customers, our authors, and Packt. Thank you!

Index

reference 21
using 17, 18, 19, 20
HTML
adding, with tag() function 11, 12
UI, creating 8, 9, 10, 11
with Shiny 5, 6, 7

I

icons
adding, to dashboard 51, 52, 53
info boxes
using 55, 56, 57

L

layout functions
about 35
flowlayout 35
fluidrow 37
navbar 37, 38, 40
navlist 37, 38, 40
sidebarlayout 35
splitlayout 36
verticallayout 36
LibreOffice application
reference 15

M

messages
adding 53, 54, 55
Movies explorer application 46

N

navbar function

about 37, 38, 40
for application layout 30
used, for creating application 30, 31, 32, 33
navlist function
about 37, 38, 40
for application layout 30
navlistPanel
used, for creating application 33, 34
notifications
adding 53, 54, 55

S

Shiny
dynamic downloadable reports 14, 15, 16, 17
support for HTML 5, 6, 7
sidebarlayout function 35
splitlayout function 36

T

tag() function
used, for adding HTML 11, 12
tasks
adding 53, 54, 55
themes
adding, to Bootstrap framework 24

U

UI
creating, with HTML 8, 9, 10, 11

V

value boxes
using 55, 56, 57
verticallayout function 36

www.ingramcontent.com/pod-product-compliance
Lightning Source LLC
Chambersburg PA
CBHW080544060326
40690CB00022B/5215